COMING TO TERMS

Coming To Terms
© Peter Sagnella / Cathexis Northwest Press

No part of this book may be reproduced without written permission of the publisher or author, except in reviews and articles.

First Printing: 2023

ISBN: 978-1-952869-80-8

Cover Art by Jeanette Compton
Design, Editing & Layout by C. M. Tollefson
Cathexis Northwest Press

cathexisnorthwestpress.com

COMING TO TERMS

POEMS BY
PETER SAGNELLA

Cathexis Northwest Press

For Marika

TABLE OF CONTENTS

Beginning Thirty Six Weeks	1
Firstborn	2
Blazed	3
Aubade	4
Fishing Hole	5
Tilling	6
Design or Coincidence	7
Old World	8
The Sod Hatch	9
The Pumpkin	10
Coming to Terms	11
Bodies	12
Crosswalk	13
After the Department of Environmental Protection Felled a Healthy Pasture Tree	14
Saxifrage	15
Dutchman's Breeches	16
Coyotes	17
A Methodical Lust	18
Woodcock Watch, Holy Thursday	19
Windfall	20
Plot	21
Bread	22
Repair	23
Till	24
Growth Rings	25

BEGINNING THIRTY-SIX WEEKS

Slung over the moat
between rib and hip
my hand guards your belly.
After, when we pulled

from the breakdown,
this same hand, knuckles
pale as sky, clamped
the wheel. You said

you could have wept.
I could have, too.
You didn't, though,
you said, because

your mother had planned
the shower for months.
        In one second
a car swerved into

our life. It swerved back,
but instead of straightening,
going forward, it planed
into a guardrail.

A bumper exploded,
bare limbs (it's too early
for buds) turned black.
No—my life didn't flash

before my eyes. Rather,
the world slowed
so each incomprehensible
moment became

comprehensible, one
flowing into the other
like the air that lifts
my hand with your belly.

FIRSTBORN

Ilulissat, the narrator says. *Mother of all glaciers.*
        I want to stop the film, tell you

to look, see—but you are in bed with our
        firstborn, nursing. The night before

you delivered we tried to watch another film—
        halfway through your water broke,

streamed down your thigh, pooled like a moulin
        on black and white laminate tile.

You laughed in semi-darkness until tears
        breached the shores of your eyelids.

I did not know then whether they were tears
        of joy, or fear.

                Tonight the house
is still, a lake at dusk. Our bedroom wall, like a dike,

separates us. The television flashes snowflake blue
        and I listen when the narrator continues.

Ilulissat, it is believed, birthed the iceberg that sank
        the Titanic. It has calved more in nine years

than it has in one hundred. Chunks of ice bigger
than a building slip. Meltwater gushes

in a long canal. I imagine you on the other side—
        skin to skin, our son's cheek warm in the valley

of your nape. Later you will wake, nurse again.
        Half-asleep, dazed, I will try to deliver

what I know is coming. But words, like air under ice
        or a child breeched, will not release.

BLAZED

When I was four we hiked West Rock with lunch—beans, hotdogs,
hot chocolate—and made fire from wads of The Journal Courier
and The New Haven Register and slats of grape boxes from California.
Heading south the trail was not blazed, and hardwood hung above us

in skeletons of twig and branch. Dad and I hugged trap rock ledges,
twisted through Oak and Hickory until we found the charred stone,
the rusted grill. High on the ridge late morning was raw. Milk
and salt warmed my throat.

                        Today, memory igniting, I hike with you.
We duck under cedar limbs, sniff resin, spot deer scat. We follow
red and blue marks on rocks and trees and veer north, northeast, south—
behold what must seem to you the edge of the world.

On smooth sloping sandstone we look out. A breeze picks up. You ask
to sit on my lap. I pull you in, wrap my arms around yours. I squeeze
you, embrace bone and the muscle attached to that bone. Your body
is warm, your cheek cold.

AUBADE

This morning, our boy berthed in bed,
I thought of you, Laertes: again hefting
foot to stone, climbing the terrace
to prune, graft a day. My bare, calloused feet
creaked the pine tread, pitched an echo
into sea-green walls. At the landing
I turned and flicked the switch—
not a wave from the harbor of his room.
Still. *Still.* Nonetheless, I knew he was sailing.

Outside dawn began its sack, pillage.
Inside shades bulwarked the wine-dark light.
Islands of song, whirlpools: I thought
of all that is to come, pulled a sheet
to his neck like some tide raiding a shore.

FISHING HOLE

When I arrive there is a knot of boys
not yet old enough to tie their own knots.

They whisper about bass, pumpkin fish,
squeal when they say the word *Snappy*.

I see none but do see a few Painters—
they float to the glint of my line as it

knifes the green and stippling surface.
I cast—slowly the knot loosens,

frays into paddleboats, bullfrogs,
cannonballs in the chlorinated pool.

       I cast again. My line lifts, arcs,
sinks, and I reel against the current.

The six-hooked, plastic minnow spins,
twists, follows the lead of my fingers.

Suddenly years swim the stony bottom—
the first cast, stiff wristed, forgetting

to let go, the August morning I found
a mother *Snappy*, beached and sprawled

like an infant, her upturned, maggot-white
belly already unraveled in the sun.

TILLING

      The promise in spring
was first fissures:

      light that splintered chinks
in warped boards,

      a dirt floor thawing like a pond,
stabs of gasoline, manure.

      In a rifting, acrid blackness,
I waited the shaping.

      Outside the shed, sharp
under dawn's nimbus,

      fumes spiraled like nebulae,
harrows wheeled like galaxies.

      He stood ready, set
by the machine, to gash. Together

      they clawed rime-splotched earth
while I followed

      with windfall stick
poking into clods, feeling surfaces

      break, dark clots of matter
that would one day

      burst into loam.

DESIGN OR COINCIDENCE

It's what she asked us, juniors in the public school,
when we tried to make literature and its language sensible.
Eyes the very particles of provocation, hair white
as the wings of springing Pegasus, how, and whom,
she taught: Hawthorne and Whitman and Dickinson
and James. Steinbeck and Melville and Twain.
Ignominy, retribution, remonstrance—words
became photons, waves. How suddenly and strangely
she came to me tonight as I tidied the kitchen,
swept crumbs and dirt from the corners,
gathered them to the center of our red oak floor,
swabbed them so they were what they weren't before.

OLD WORLD

Days like these, sky grim as the eyes of Hades,
he led me over heaps of grape skin, past the wine press,
and into the fields. Up the dam I trailed him, watching
the knife snug in wooden hoops that belted staves.
We hiked on Clover, Trefoil, Vetch, past seed now,
tufted and fanning like headdresses. The path hooked
under bramble near Pine, and we entered there
to hunt Nailheads. Down the ridge around rotting logs
or trunks of Hickory were studded caps. Pluck by pluck
the blade lopped. Our bushel filled with these, earth's
dankest Persephone, left stems like fleshless fingers
of exhumed warrior kings. Years later, reading, I learned
the word *mycelium*, was rapt by what it was, what
its sound called up, a civilization underground.

THE SOD HATCH

We buried you in the morning, listening
In silence to thrums from the Interstate,
Buffets of wind that slapped blouses and shirts,
Shallow stabs of the gravedigger turning
A sod hatch onto your urn. When he tipped
The last spade he murmured *That's all she wrote*
And our island became archipelago.
In the distance, the immutable
Mausoleum: varved tombs of pink granite.

That afternoon, readying the garden,
I sank my spade into the bin, piled
Shovelful on shovelful like foothills
In a range. Raked the hills into plains,
Sifted midden, decaying from decayed.

THE PUMPKIN

In September we carried it from my parents' porch
and placed it on ours. It was an orange star then,
and it was summer. Coming home every day
was coming home to the sun. Columbus Day
we bought Mums—yellow, rust—and three
scarecrows. Tuesday, however, squirrels burrowed
a cleft, and by Thursday our pumpkin sank
to concrete. Sunday, clutching a coal shovel, I scraped
skin and flesh, lay both on the compost. Later,
hands bare, raked pulp into palm, juice draining
between fingers, seeds pale as the eyes of a dead child—
I carried these to the compost as well. There, sun
carving wind and cloud, I thought I saw vine and leaf
and flower, blood-red, gold, crawl into light.

COMING TO TERMS

When the first quarter was almost finished,
a day with sky gray, deep as a vault,
we broke from our routine testing of words.
Thanatopsis, she mused. *A View to Death*.

The dark green tomb of a chalk slate.
Desks rowed like a field of headstones.
A Xeroxed sheet jambed by black blots.
Throaty, tremulous, she meted grave

sounds between long, regenerative pauses.
The lines pranced, were mute as globed fruit.
In the spaces we waited for dead women
and men to rise like Lazarus, call to our door.

But these cessations resurrected no one.
Rather we in the silences transcribed what rose
within ourselves, revised the lives
we thought we knew. And what words

came to? *Lips pressed to skulls. Cheeks sallow,
thin. Cold beads, stiff hands. Mouths sewn shut.*

BODIES

From the pew I watch as she ministers
the body, black cross tucked in the hollow

of her chest. The psalmist hymns
Shepherd me, O Lord, from death into life.

One by one to her they move, corpus
of grief. I see their mouths open and wait,

and remember the pull of that body—
stooping under cross and crown

and halo, waiting for bread to conflate
with the tongue. One in one, mouthing

a language of suffering, a chronicle
of bearing life's burden.

       Not stooping now to genuflection,
I listen as she repeats *The Body of Christ*

and watch mouths close, assuaged.
High on the dais she has to stoop once

to slip the wafer between two parched lips—
and I see her stooping in the chancel

of her room, her frail, forgetful mother
resisting any plea to rise from bed.

She strawed water between those lips then
as if with a reed of vinegar and hyssop.

And I see the way our bodies go,
their need to rise again, their need to stoop.

CROSSWALK

As in Rothko, white panes dissolve
then surface, become stepping stones,
ford for us a river of tarmac. On the other

shore an eye floats, flashes a shepherd's
ghost, a fleshy, spike-less palm. At the
blacktopped fork I ask what's the way—
you say *to brook*.
                              Once there we talk
of what we see: current rising, falling,
twigs of thorn, root cradles, forsaken
by flood. Behind us Cedar forks sunlight.

Then we spot a Pine, blown down, a bridge
fording the brook. Snapped branches lance
the trunk like crucifixes—we climb, clasp

the rotted ends for handholds, totter
to the tree's heart. I strain there to see
if you'll let go, but abandon never spikes
in your palm.

AFTER THE DEPARTMENT OF ENVIRONMENTAL PROTECTION FELLED A HEALTHY PASTURE TREE

When this spring
the buds awaken
go where years before

you have gone:
woodland trilling,
blue-grey lake,

the pasture. Carry
your burden
on dampening field

where they buried
Red Maple, Quaking Aspen.
Feel in limbo there

branches and bark
underfoot. Climb
the greening hill

as if Golgotha knelled
a death, as if a cross
was chopped, stumped.

SAXIFRAGE

Saxum frangere—to break stone.

You know in this could root a parable:
The poor overcoming the rich,
The meek fracturing the strong.
The lithic heart, warns Sophocles, cracks first—

But high on this basaltic ridge, above
The leafless, eroded river valley,
Any warm wind seems beat back by rock.
Six thousand years ago they hunted, camped,

Gathered in that valley. They quarried
The flaked Quartzite you clench now in fingers.
Loosen your grip: the shards might fashion
In the crevice of your palm a rosette,

A stem, a cairn of white petals.

DUTCHMAN'S BREECHES

And there they were, just
as the field guide described:

Pale pantaloons, upside down,
billowing, as if hung to dry on a line.

Rocking and tossing, never
quite at ease. Pockets gold, cupped

like open palms. Each time
you spotted them on the well-worn

trail the going was slow: you knelt,
crouched, started and stopped like one

charting what he wished to leave
uncharted. They were bear claws.

Extracted teeth. Nike's arms
stretched to victory. Wolf legs

wire-strung outside a trapper's
cabin. But always, always,

they were the *Onrust's* white sails
puffing, thrusting up the coast.

COYOTES

In the dark long ago I heard the howl.
Upridge, whorls of sound above

Mad Mare Hill. Like nostrils sniffing
an unwanted scent I could turn then

from that contour of night, let ear
and eye shape a day's bright chant.

Then in brilliant sunset gleam I saw
one trot across a field, teeth clenched,

jaw firm, locked like a sentinel's
spotlighting the black for an uprising.

Dead, the rabbit knew nothing
of the power in that jaw. Or perhaps,

in its way, in its final frantic fury,
it knew all.

To rise up. Once
you told us the story: how they shot

any villager who tried to feed a family
on greens picked in the fields of Papoulia.

From the bough of one tree they hung
the bodies, then dumped them in holes

of hot, parched earth. At night, you said,
keen to the scent, a pack came to feed.

It tore, ripped corpses from the dirt.
By morning half-gnawed, tissue-flecked

bones had surfaced like snapped riggings
of sunk ships. And whenever you inhaled

the sweet leaf of that tree, you could not
keep its stench out of your throat.

A METHODICAL LUST

Once I saw them huddle on a long, dead branch,
a coven of black backs humped and silent
in failing light. Another time, summer,
they lined three and four on thick Fir boughs—
statuesque, quiet, gazing and waiting
like sable robed judges. No rage, no contempt,
nothing in that August air said they gorge
the sweetbread of power. But up close
today I knew those solemn watches portage
a patient, methodical lust. For half an hour
one picked and tugged a mound of fur, seized
bloody innards like a ferryman seizing
tickets on a pier. Beak deft as fingertips,
soot-black wings taut, poised as the oar of Charon.

WOODCOCK WATCH, HOLY THURSDAY

We stand in one row at the stubby edge
of marsh and field, as if testifying
before a congregation. The sky into which

we gaze is an altar—clear, cobalt, cold—
and we try not to face the north wind
that sweeps the greening hills. I wait

for last light to vanish, clutch the binoculars
hanging from my neck like a cross, remember:
the evening mass at our neighborhood church,

the priest, inverting his power, kneeling
to wash the feet of stonemasons, carpenters,
plumbers. I try to recall the theme of the prayer

in Gethsemane—deliverance, resignation—
but our guide begins to talk. He says the bill
is long, adapted perfectly to this nesting place

and the diet of worms it provides. He says
the earthy plumage, too, camouflages
deftly in marsh like this. Wind dies.

Silence hovers. We can do nothing but wait,
so I glance to our guide for some direction
but, teeth gritted, face paling, he too seems displaced.

Then his eyes leave the purpling horizon
and his flashlight cuts the edge of the field.
A tuft of Rye becomes a halo. In this light

a small head twitches, a black eye beads.
We hear a nasally buzz, a communion call,
our guide prophesy, "Here he goes." Wings

flutter, a body lifts, becomes a rising blur
in the dark. Again and again he spirals the edge
of this territory and we, stuck on it, eyes nailed

to sky, again and again wait for an ascension.

WINDFALL

Day after day, the winter before he died,
he sat in front of a fieldstone hearth.

None of what he burned he split. They were gifts
from the neighbor: burled, gnarled, cankerous

chunks that fell long ago when the lot
next door was field. Aspen, Red Maple,

even Russian Olive. Sometimes, before the sun
sank below the ridge or the cold yellowed

the ends of his fingers, he hobbled down
the drive, the day's exercise. Bent for the paper,

dropped the mailbox door. Maybe once,
maybe twice, always afraid a knife of wind

would slice him down, knowing his spine
was rotting already from the inside.

PLOT

Twist, I think now, staring at your grave—
the way you waited with scrubbed face

and clean hair, eyes bright with the news.
Rising from a chair, you reached

for the walker, shuffled to the table,
opened a binder that held the pages

      of your life. *The Factory Section*,
you called it: sketches of New Haven,

vignettes of your sister, father, brother,
mother, composed as chapters in a book.

And how we, weeks later, tried to compose
the final chapter—home hospice bed

delivered, papers signed—in the house
you dreamed, built, but could not die in.

BREAD

Hers were working hands, palms supple, thick,
Fingers trim as seams she stitched to patch quilts.

Sundays with our own we broke her bread—
Honeycombed, dense, nothing like the wafer—

Levered thin brown crust with forefinger
And thumb, wiped plates clean of her gleaning.

      Her lips never hymned *manifest destiny*
But those fingers knew it: the stick or the spring,

The floury wave, the cold mass that waited.
East and west she stretched, north, south.

When she died, knuckles braided in repose,
Hospital room warm as a kitchen, word-loaves

Broke upon on our lips, were the only holy
Offering: *la famiglia sta qua, la famiglia sta qua.*

REPAIR

When he could not sleep he sought this room,
conditioned by the comfort, the years spent.
Only this place delayed the pain and gloom,
the thought he was beginning the end.
Then, midsummer, he died. Fall came round
and I started to work, tear out what he built—
studs and joists, jambs, plates. Piled on the ground.
Shingles rotted soft as a homemade quilt.
With his old saw I ripped boards to length,
reframed the wall, rehung the window
in the corner where he slept. Found a strength
in joining what has gone to what will go:
the floor on which he found a last reprieve,
the foundation under with its crack, heave.

TILL

With an old hoe
from his father's shed
he rakes compost

over screen tacked
to rails of a gray spruce
gate. What remains

of the year cascades
a hundred wire casements
and a barrow of dirt.

This dirt he works:
pulls crowns, pricks

sand and root, pushes
snags of hay or leaf
until what remains

is more till than tide,
rising with unearthly
swiftness into moraine

and drumlin, months
of shell, rind, skin now
for the bone of earth.

GROWTH RINGS

When I set the lanced teeth into pitch
It was like ripping skin. Steel tips
Scraping the kerf, razor edges tearing
Cambium and pith, then cambium and pitch.

With a looping cut my shoulder rocked
Down and through. Then, no one ready,
The trunk splintered, opened. Boughs rammed
Ice-clods, shuddered on hoar-tipped leaves.

That a month ago. New Year's I dragged it
Unornamented through whitewashed jambs.
In the garden now it lays supine, felled
By that which it never saw coming.

And now, squatting in tense reflection,
I lower myself to observe the pith.
Trace the burred edge, funnel my nail
Into nine years that girdle a first.

Your nave pops, cambium pushes
Plates of bark. My fingertips spiral
Your skin-sheath, needles photosynthesize.
Pith within pith, force centripetal, I rise

To sense. Circles are what we marry.
A star system. Core of water, light.
Belly swelling with possibility.
Round striations against wind and blight.

The writer thanks the editors of the following journals and websites where these poems first appeared:

Noctua: Beginning Thirty Six Weeks
Naugatuck River Review: Old World
Connecticut River Review: Design or Coincidence
Rust and Moth: The Sod Hatch
Common Ground: The Pumpkin
Pinyon: Growth Rings
Connecticut Woodlands: Blazed
Plainsongs: Till
Borderlands: After the Department of Environmental Protection
    Felled a Healthy Pasture Tree
Kestrel: Bread
SLANT: Saxifrage
The Comstock Review: Aubade
Cold Mountain Review: Coyotes
Cathexis Northwest Press: Tilling
Wild Roof: A Methodical Lust
Cagibi: Repair
New Limestone Review: Firstborn, Woodcock Watch, Holy Thursday,
    Windfall

Peter Sagnella lives with his wife and sons in North Haven, Connecticut, where he has taught Composition, Poetry, and Environmental Literature for twenty-two years. A Pushcart nominee and Edwin Way Teale Writer-in-Residence, his work has been exhibited at the Yale School of Forestry and appeared in many journals, most recently *Wild Roof, Cagibi, New Limestone Review,* and *Shō*.

Also Available from Cathexis Northwest Press:

Something To Cry About
by Robert Krantz

Suburban Hermeneutics
by Ian Cappelli

God's Love Is Very Busy
by David Seung

that one time we were almost people
by Christian Czaniecki

Fever Dream/Take Heart
by Valyntina Grenier

The Book of Night & Waking
by Clif Mason

Dead Birds of New Zealand
by Christian Czaniecki

The Weathering of Igneous Rockforms in High-Altitude Riparian Environments
by John Belk

If A Fish
by George Burns

How to Draw a Blank
by Collin Van Son

En Route
by Jesse Wolfe

sky bright psalms
by Temple Cone

Moonbird
by Henry G. Stanton

southern athiest. oh, honey
by d. e. fulford

Bruises, Birthmarks & Other Calamities
by Nadine Klassen

Wanted: Comedy, Addicts
by AR Dugan

They Curve Like Snakes
by David Alexander McFarland

the catalog of daily fears
by Beth Dufford

Shops Close Too Early
by Josh Feit

Vanity Unfair and Other Poems
by Robert Eugene Rubino

Destructive Heresies
by Milo E. Gorgevska

Bodies of Separation
by Chim Sher Ting

The Night with James Dean and Other Prose Poems
by Allison A. deFreese

About Time
by Julie Benesh

Suspended
by Ellen White Rook

The Unempty Spaces Between
by Louis Efron

Quomodo probatur in conflatorio
by Nick Roberts

Call Me Not Ishmael but the Sea
by J. Martin Daughtry

Wild Evolution
by Naomi Leimsider

Acta
by Patrick Wilcox

Cathexis Northwest Press